My toys

What's this? / What are these?

Write questions and answers.

1

What's this?

It's a boat.

2

What are these?

They're cars.

3

4

1 How many ...

2 Unscramble. Then write and answer.

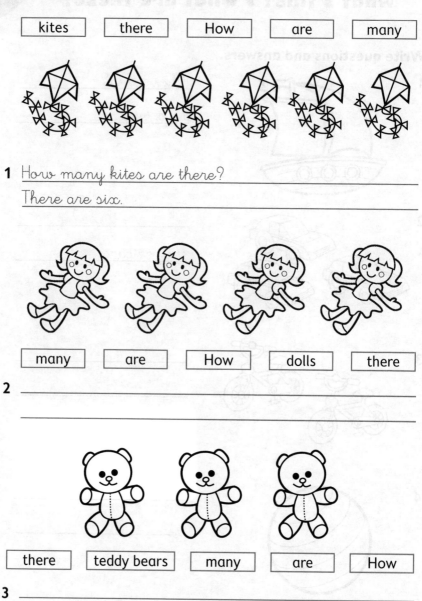

| kites | there | How | are | many |

1 How many kites are there?
There are six.

| many | are | How | dolls | there |

2 _____

_____

| there | teddy bears | many | are | How |

3 _____

_____

Read the answers. Then write the questions and draw.

1 <u>What are these?</u>
   <u>How many books are there?</u>

They're books.
There are three.

2 <u>What's this?</u>
   <u>How many boats are there?</u>

It's a boat.
There's one.

3 _____

They're cars.
There are two.

4 _____

It's a train.
There's one.

Write the contraction.

1 It is a bus.   <u>It's a bus.</u>

2 They are bikes.   <u>They're bikes.</u>

3 What is this?   _____

4 There is one.   _____

5 It is a lorry.   _____

My family

Who's he / she?

1 **Look and read. Then answer. Use words from the word box.**

cousin	brother	sister	aunt	~~uncle~~

```
        ┌─────────┐   ┌──────────┐
        │ Granny  │───│ Grandad  │
        └─────────┘   └──────────┘
```

Seb		Louise		Dad		Mum

Tina		Me	Anne	James

1 Who's Seb?   <u>He's my uncle.</u>

2 Who's James?   _____

3 Who's Louise?   _____

4 Who's Anne?   _____

5 Who's Tina?   _____

2 **Look and match. Then write.**

1 Uncle Jim		**a** living room
2 my brother		**b** kitchen
3 my sister		**c** bedroom
4 my granny		**d** bathroom

1 Where's Uncle Jim? _____

2 _____ She's in the bedroom.

3 Where's my granny? _____

4 _____ He's in the bathroom.

3 **Find the sentences. Then draw.**

4	's	the	on	there	cat	table
3	on	there	you	next	sofa	to
2	a	~~are~~	lamps	you	chair	two
1	~~there~~	a	sofa	the	the	's
	A	B	C	D	E	F

1

There	are					
A1	B2	F2	C2	C4	B4	F4

2

There						
B3	A4	A2	E2	D3	F3	E1	C1

3

There						
D4	F1	B1	E4	A3	D1	E3

Move your body

Touch your toes

Match the words.

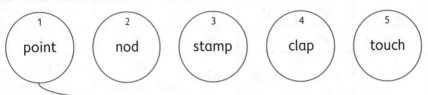

1	2	3	4	5
point	nod	stamp	clap	touch

a	b	c	d	e
feet	head	hands	toes	fingers

Write sentences. Use the prompts.

1 Tom can't touch his toes. _____ (Tom / can't / touch / toes)

2 _____ (you / can / point / fingers)

3 _____ (Sara / can't / nod / head)

4 _____ (I / can / clap / hands)

5 _____ (he / can't / stamp / feet)

What can you do? Write sentences.

✔	✘
1 I can touch my toes.	2 I can't clap my hands.
3	4
5	6

4 Complete the questions. Then look and answer.

Mum	✔	✔	✘	✔	✔
Dad	✔	✔	✔	✘	✘
Granny	✔	✘	✔	✘	✘
Grandad	✔	✔	✘	✘	✘
	swim	climb	swing	do cartwheels	stand on your head

1 _Can_____ Granny do cartwheels? _No, she can't._____

2 _____ Grandad swing? _____

3 _____ Mum Climb? _____

4 _____ Dad Stand on his head? _____

5 _____ Granny swim? _____

5 Write sentences with can't.

1 _Grandad can't stand on his head.___

2 Granny _____ .

3 Mum _____ .

4 Dad _____ .

5 I _____ .

Look. Then unscramble and write.

1 ball / I / a / kick / can

<u>I can kick a ball.</u>

2 can / I / the / splits / do

_____

3 can / head / stand / my / I / on

_____

4 fast / run / can / I

_____

5 high / can / jump / I

_____

4 My face

I've got short hair

1 Complete the web. Use the words in the word box

brown	brown	blue	curly	long
straight	big	small	dark	blond

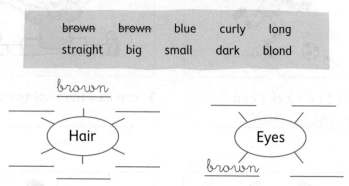

brown

Hair

Eyes

brown

2 Write new sentences.

1 Tom has got dark hair. *His hair is dark.*

2 His hair is long. *He's got long hair.*

3 His eyes are big. _____

4 Lucy has got curly hair. _____

3 Answer the questions about you.

1 Have you got long brown hair? *Yes, I have. / No, I haven't.*

2 Have you got big blue eyes? _____

3 Have you got a small straight nose? _____

4 Have you got curly brown hair? _____

4 Look. Then write sentences about the people.

Mum
Mum is on the sofa.
She's got long hair. Her
hair is blond and straight.
Her hair is neat.
She's got big eyes.

Dad

My little brother

My sister

5 **Unscramble and write. Then draw.**

| square | She's | heads | two | got |

1 _____ .

| are | fingers | long | and | straight | Her |

2 _____ .

| Her | triangle | big | nose | a | is |

3 _____ .

Animals 5

What's this / that?

1 Circle the correct words.

1 (What's)/ What are that?

2 It's / They're a turkey.

3 It's got / It's white.

4 It's got / It's feathers.

2 Look and read. Then complete.

1 What's that?

It's a goat.

It's big.

It's white.

It's got four legs and a tail.

2 What _____

_____

_____

_____

_____

3 _____

_____

_____

_____

_____

5 Is it big?

3 Find the questions and answers. Then guess the animal.

an owl	a bat	hens

Is → it	Is	it	is	.	?	Yes,
? ← big	.	black	it	Has	wings	it
No, it	isn't	?	Yes,	it	got	has

1 Is it big? _____ No, it isn't. _____.

_____ ? _____ ?

_____ ? _____ ?

It's a bat! _____

Is	.	Has	it	has	.	?	Yes,
it	Yes	big	got	it	Has	wings	it
big	?	eyes	?	Yes,	it	got	has

2 _____ ? _____.

_____ ? _____.

_____ ? _____.

It's _____ !

Are → they	Are	they	are	.	?	Yes,
? big	.	brown	they	Have	wings	they
No, they	aren't	?	Yes,	they	got	have

3 _____ ? _____.

_____ ? _____.

_____ ? _____.

They're _____ !

4 Look and read. Then complete.

	duck	turkey	ostrich	cow	goat
big	✗	✗	✔	✔	✔
small	✔	✔	✗	✗	✗
brown	✗	✔	✔	✔	✔
white	✔	✗	✗	✗	✗
legs	2	2	2	4	4
wings	✔	✔	✔	✗	✗

1 The cows _are big and brown._   _They've got four legs._

2 The goats _____ . _____

3 The turkeys _____ . _____

4 The ostriches _____ . _____

5 The ducks _____ . _____

5 Look again. Then write and answer.

1 Q: _Are the ducks big?_   (ducks / big)

   A: _No, they're not. They're small._

2 Q: _Have the turkeys got wings?_   (turkeys / wings)

   A: _Yes, they have._

3 Q: _____   (ostriches / small)

   A: _____

4 Q: _____   (goats / two legs)

   A: _____

6 Food

What's your favourite food? / I like ...

1 Read. Then write the opposite.

1 I like pizza.   <u>I don't like pizza.</u>

2 Tom likes apples.   <u>   </u>

3 Dad likes salad.   <u>   </u>

4 I like chicken.   <u>   </u>

2 Unscramble. Then write and answer.

1 Do / you / chicken / like / ?

Q: <u>Do you like chicken?</u>

A: <u>   </u>

2 like / you / ? / Do / bananas

Q: <u>   </u>

A: <u>   </u>

3 mum / your / like / Does / ? / chocolate

Q: <u>   </u>

A: <u>   </u>

3 What food do you like? What food don't you like? Write.

<u>   </u>

He / She likes / doesn't like ...

4 **Look at the food in Mum's shopping bag. Read.**
Then choose *True* (T) or *False* (F).

1 She doesn't like rice.	T /(F)
2 She likes chicken.	T / F
3 She likes burgers.	T / F
4 She likes fish.	T / F
5 She doesn't like bananas.	T / F
6 She doesn't like pizza.	T / F

5 **Look again. Then write questions and answers.**

1 <u>Does Mum like bananas?</u> ? <u>No,</u> , <u>she doesn't.</u> . (bananas)

2 _____ ? ____ , _____ . (hot dogs)

3 _____ ? ____ , _____ . (pizza)

4 _____ ? ____ , _____ . (eggs)

6 some / any

6 **Circle *some* or *any*.**

1 There's (some)/ any milk.

2 There aren't *some* / *any* beans.

3 There are *some* / *any* pancakes.

4 There aren't *some* / *any* pineapples.

5 There isn't *some* / *any* rice.

7 **Write sentences. Use *some* and *any*.**

✔ milk ✘ oranges ✔ fish ✘ honey ✘ chocolate ✔ vegetables

In my kitchen ...

✔		✘	
1 There's some milk.		2 There aren't any oranges.	
3 _____ .		4 _____ .	
5 _____ .		6 _____ .	

8 **Look at the chart in Exercise 7 again. Write questions and answers.**

1 Is there any honey in your kitchen?   No, there isn't.

2 _____   _____

3 _____   _____

Clothes 7

I'm wearing / not wearing ...

1 Unscramble. Then answer about you.

1 you / ? / Are / wearing / skirt / today / a

Q: _Are you wearing a skirt today?_   A: _____ .

2 black / wearing / ? / Are / shoes / you

Q: _____ ?   A: _____ .

3 jumper / green / ? / wearing / you / Are / a

Q: _____ ?   A: _____ .

2 What are you wearing? Put (✔) or (✗). Then write and draw.

T-shirt ☐	shoes ☐
jeans ☐	coat ☐
jumper ☐	dress ☐
trainers ☐	skirt ☐
cap ☐	trousers ☐

1 ✔ _I'm wearing a dress._

2 ✗ _I'm not wearing_

3 ✔ _____

4 ✗ _____

5 ✔ _____

What would you like?

3 Unscramble and write. Then answer about you.

| blue | Would | like | coat | a | you |

1 Q: _Would you like a blue coat?_

A: _____

| shoes | like | Would | you | black |

2 Q: _____

A: _____

4 Read the list. Then complete the conversation.

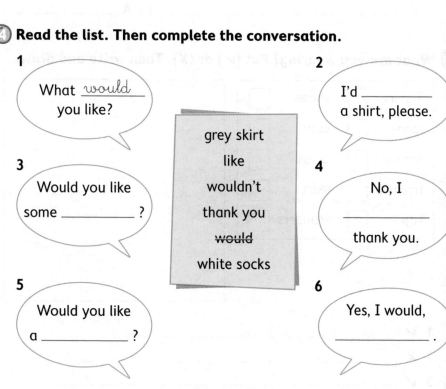

1
What _would_
you like?

2
I'd _____
a shirt, please.

3
Would you like
some _____ ?

4
No, I
_____
thank you.

grey skirt
like
wouldn't
thank you
~~would~~
white socks

5
Would you like
a _____ ?

6
Yes, I would,
_____ .

5 Put the words in the chart.

~~trainers~~ T-shirt dress socks jacket skirt trousers
~~shoes~~ hat jeans glasses jumper coat

at school	*shoes*
on holiday	*trainers*

6 You are at school. What are you wearing? Draw. Then write.

I'm wearing

7 You are on holiday. What are you wearing? Draw. Then write.

8 Weather

What's the weather like?

1 Look. Then read and match.

a

b

c

d

1 It's rainy. `c`

2 It's stormy. ☐

3 It's windy. ☐

4 It's snowy. ☐

2 Look at the symbols. Then write.

1   *it's cold and snowy.*

2   _____ .

3   _____ .

4   _____ .

This kite is mine

3 Read. Then complete the sentences.

1 This is my kite. It's _mine_ .

2 That's your snowman. It's _____ .

3 These are her keys. They are _____ .

4 That's his snowman. It's _____ .

5 This is her pencil case. It's _____ .

6 These are my hot dogs. They're _____ .

4 Read. Then complete. Use words from the word box.

hers ~~mine~~

yours mine

yours

It's windy today. I can fly my kite. Look – this kite is ¹_mine_ .
It's red and yellow. Hey, Tom! That's Sue's kite. It's blue and white.
It isn't ²_____ , it's ³_____ ! ⁴_____ is red and
orange – it's over there. I think ⁵_____ is the most beautiful!

5 Write questions and answers. Use the prompts.

1 _Do you like cloudy days?_ (cloudy days) _No, I don't._ (✘)

2 _____ (hot days) _____ (✔)

3 _____ (windy days) _____ (✘)

6 **Unscramble. Then write.**

1 weather / What's / like / the / December / in

Sara: <u>What's the weather like in December?</u>

2 cold / is / It / wet / and

Tom: _____ .

3 months / hot / Which / are / country / your / in

Sara: _____ ?

4 hot / July / August / are / country / in / my / and

Tom: _____ .

5 favourite / month / is / Which / your

Sara: _____ ?

7 **Complete the calendar with the months. Then put the weather in for your country. Use the words in the box.**

snowy	stormy	windy	hot	rainy	sunny	cold

	Month	Weather
1	January February <u>March</u>	<u>snowy cold</u>
2	April _____ June	_____
3	July August _____	_____
4	_____ November December	_____